Timberlake Wertenbaker's plays include *The Grace of Mary Traverse* (Royal Court, main stage, London, 1985), *Our Country's Good* (Royal Court, main stage, London and Broadway), winner of the Laurence Olivier Play of the Year Award in 1988 and the New York Drama Critics' Circle Award for Best New Foreign Play in 1991, *The Love of the Nightingale* (Royal Shakespeare Company's Other Place, Stratford-upon-Avon), which won the 1989 Eileen Anderson Central TV Drama Award, *Three Birds Alighting on a Field* (Royal Court, main stage, London), which won the Susan Smith Blackburn Award, Writers' Guild Award and London Critics' Circle Award in 1992, *The Break of Day* (Out of Joint production, Royal Court, London, and touring, 1995), *After Darwin* (Hampstead Theatre, London, 1998) and *Dianeira* (Catherine Bailey productions, Radio 3, 1999). She has written the screenplay of *The Children*, based on Edith Wharton's novel, and a BBC2 film entitled *Do Not Disturb*. Translations include Marivaux's *La Dispute*, Jean Anouilh's *Leocadia*, Maurice Maeterlinck's *Pelleas and Melisande* for BBC Radio, Ariane Mnouchkine's *Mephisto*, adapted for the RSC in 1986, Sophocles' *The Theban Plays* (RSC, London and Stratford, 1991), Euripides' *Hecuba* (ACT, San Francisco, 1995), Eduardo de Filippo's *Filumena* (Piccadilly Theatre, 1999) and Pirandello's *Come tu me vuoi*.

TIMBERLAKE WERTENBAKER

The Ash Girl

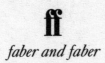

faber and faber

First published in 2000
by Faber and Faber Limited
3 Queen Square, London WC1N 3AU
Published in the United States by Faber and Faber Inc.
an affiliate of Farrar, Straus and Giroux, New York

Typeset by Country Setting, Kingsdown, Kent CT14 8ES
Printed in England by Mackays of Chatham plc, Chatham, Kent

A CIP record for this book
is available from the British Library

ISBN 0–571–20942–4

2 4 6 8 10 9 7 5 3 1

For Dushka

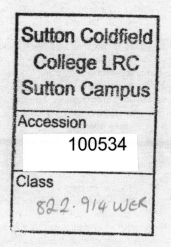

The Ash Girl was first presented at Birmingham Repertory Theatre on 8 December 2000. The cast, in order of appearance, was as follows:

Ruth Jane Cameron
Judith Rachel Smith
Ashgirl Stephanie Pochin
Mother Vivien Parry
Princess Zehra Souad Faress
Prince Amir Justin Avoth
Paul Huss Garbiya
Slothworm Alex Jones
Angerbird Tracy Wiles
Envysnake/Owl Kenn Sabberton
Gluttontoad/Fairy Darlene Johnson
Pridefly/Spider Jonathan Bond
Greedmonkey/Otter Togo Igawa
Sadness Sarah Coomes
Lust Emma Lowndes
Man in the Forest Ken Shorter
Girlmouse
Boymouse

Director Lucy Bailey
Designer Angela Davies
Lighting Designer Chahini Yavroyan
Composer Orlando Gough
Choreographer Michael Dolan

Characters

in order of appearance

Ruth
Judith
Ashgirl
Mother
Princess Zehra
Prince Amir
Paul
Slothworm
Angerbird
Envysnake
Gluttontoad
Pridefly
Greedmonkey
Sadness
Lust
Man in the Forest
Owl
Otter
Fairy in the Mirror
Girlmouse
Boymouse

The house, the palace, the forest

THE ASH GIRL

Act One

SCENE ONE
WHO LIVES IN THE HOUSE

*The breakfast room of a dilapidated medieval-type
house. A very large hearth, thickly blanketed with ashes.
A massive sideboard, laden with foods.*
    The room is dark.
    *Ruth and Judy enter. As they come in, there is a
movement in the ashes, a ripple, no more.*
    *The two girls skip to and from the sideboard, lifting
the heavy silver covers and helping themselves with glee.*

Ruth Chicken.

Judith Pigeon.

Ruth Casseroled pheasant.

Judith Boiled swan.

Ruth Wild boar.

Judith Pig's ears with juniper berries.

Ruth Clotted cream.

Judith And damson jam.

Ruth I feel full.

Judith I feel fat.

Ruth Mother says we must be thin.

Judith Why?

Ruth Because girls must be thin.

Judith Why?

Ruth How *do* you get thin?

Judith You stop eating.

Ruth Stop eating damson jam! Swan and sausages? Never.

Judith We could start getting thin tomorrow. Today, I want an unboring day.

Ruth We could practise our dancing.

Judith Boring. I want a good gallop over the fields.

Ruth Father took away the last horse.

Judith Took the horse and vanished.

Ruth Into thin air.

Judith Into a bear.

Ruth A thin, a hairy, a grizzly bear.

Judith Waits in his lair . . .

They burst out laughing. A movement in the ashes.

Ruth We could read a book.

Judith I'm bored with happy endings. Why should everybody live happily ever after? Why can't the monster eat everyone?

Ruth And live very fully ever after. What about that pamphlet on manners?

Judith We don't need manners, we never see anyone.

Ruth I'd like to paint, but Mother says it makes me look a mess.

Judith I'd like to find a worm, open it and see what's inside. Open the stomach of a mouse, cut the legs off an ant and see if they move.
    I'd need one of those glasses that make everything big.

Ruth There's one in father's study, shall we take it?

A movement in the ashes.

Judith Mother keeps the key: wait till she's asleep, steal the key, take everything out of the study. That would be very unboring.

Ruth When he finds out?

Judith He's never coming back. Never never –

Ruth Ever after . . .

Judith A grizzly bear . . .

Ruth In his lair . . .

Movement in the ashes. And now a figure emerges, grey, spectral, skeletally thin, a girl of about seventeen.

Judith Ashgirl. Eyeing us.

Ruth Spying.

Judith Look and tell.

Ashgirl I will tell mother you're planning to steal the key.

They seize her arms.

Ruth You won't!

Judith She won't believe you.

Ashgirl I always tell the truth.

Ruth It's the way you tell it!

Judith Boring. Very boring. Lies are more interesting.

Ashgirl How can the truth be boring? Father admonished me always to tell the truth.

Ruth And where is he now?

Judith The grizzly bear . . .

Ashgirl Stop it!

The girls laugh.

Ruth Come on, Ashie, have some breakfast.

Ashgirl No thank you.

Ruth Food in this house not good enough for you?

Judith Growing girl must eat.

Ashgirl tries to return to the ashes, but Judith takes a sausage, hands it to Ashgirl.

Take it!

Ashgirl shakes her head.
Ruth takes a scone, lots of cream and jam. Proffers it.

Ruth When your sisters offer, you accept, you say thank you.

Ashgirl I don't want anything.

Ruth Book says: bad manners to refuse a gift. I like books which tell other people what to do.

They wait. Ashgirl looks at the food in disgust.

Judith Eat!

Ruth She's so rude.

Judith Stuff it in her mouth.

Ruth grinds the scone in Ashgirl's mouth. She gags, spits, more grinding, more violent. Judith eats the sausage, calmly.

I could eat a fried pig's heart.

Ruth (*to Ashgirl, on the floor*) Lick the crumbs. Say sorry.

They pin her down.

Judith That's compulsory.

Ruth Conclusory.

Judith Persuasory.

Ruth We're waiting.

Judith Maybe another scone? Gnawed bone of swan?

Ashgirl Sorry . . .

Ruth Sorry for?

Ashgirl Sorry – for – for being – me.

They let her go. A moment.

Ruth The thing is, Ashie, if you were nicer to us, we'd be nicer to you.

The girls leave, Ashgirl sinks back into the ashes.

SCENE TWO
WHO LIVES IN THE ASHES

Ashgirl I don't remember much. It was another countryside, another country. Green. Flowers inside. My mother loved flowers.

I don't know when she died, if she died. I was always with my father. He was my friend. I am your friend for ever, he said. He took me everywhere, travels, hunting, I sat under castle tables and listened to the men talk. We slept on his cloak in the woods, naming the stars.

Until we came here. First for an afternoon, then a night, then days, and finally to stay. He never told me he wanted to marry her, he didn't even ask me, his friend. And that these girls would be his daughters, call themselves my sisters. He said he loved me most, but he needed, needed, and I was growing up – but he loved me.

He wasn't happy long. I saw lines of loneliness return to his face. I went to him, but he'd become afraid. He was strange, he wasn't my friend. He told me he was not a good man, he had monsters to fight. I said I would fight them with him, but he said no, these monsters were different, they'd poisoned the blood to his heart and I must forgive him. And so he went in search of his heart and broke mine.

And that's when I found the ashes. Ashes are warm and in the ashes no one sees you, you do no wrong. Ashes on your head, no one talks to you, ashes on your arms, no one touches you, ashes are safe. And I will stay in these ashes, melt into them, shrink to their weightlessness. Cloak of crumbling grey. My ashes.

SCENE THREE
WHO GOES TO THE BALL

The Mother comes in. She is held back, neat, straight. The girls follow her. She holds a large golden scroll in her hand.

Mother I hoped it was from my husband, gifts, money. It's an invitation – addressed to all the daughters of the house.

Judith/Ruth We are the daughters of the house.

Ruth We haven't been anywhere all winter.

Mother You mustn't be seen with the wrong people.

Judith What are wrong people?

Mother When there's no father, people talk.

Ruth Let me read it.

Mother It's addressed to all the daughters of the house. (*She makes a gesture towards the ashes.*)

Ruth I'm the oldest.

Judith But I'm clever.

They both snatch at the scroll.

Mother You can have a look too, Ashgirl.

Ashgirl (*from the ashes*) I'm not interested.

Mother It is to all my daughters.

Ashgirl (*emerging from the ashes*) I'm not your daughter!

Mother Clean yourself up. You look disgusting. And you've got crumbs all over your face.

Ashgirl I'll clear the breakfast.

Mother Judith and Ruth can help you.

Ashgirl I like to do it myself.

Mother You don't help yourself, Ashgirl. I've heard people whispering I'm not nice to you, but I try.

Ruth and Judith are unrolling the scroll. The decoration is ornate, golds and browns.

Ruth 'You are invited . . . '

Mother That paper is too bright.

Judith The letters are of gold.

Mother People shouldn't show off.

Judith 'To dance . . . '

Mother Is it real gold?

Ruth 'At the palace of . . . '

Mother A palace . . .

Ruth 'Princess Zehra.'

Mother A princess!

Ruth 'In honour of her son, Prince Amir's . . . '

Mother Amir?

Ruth 'Birthday on' – it's next week!

Judith We don't have any ball gowns.

Mother It's not a local name, they're foreigners.

Ruth A prince!

Mother That's always interesting. And rich. But foreign.

Judith He could be from Araby.

Mother Everyone important will be there, we have to go.

Ruth What are we going to wear ?

Mother A normal responsible father would have heard of this ball and sent rich cloths, shoes of brocade. It seems we'll have to manage with some old gowns of mine.

Ashgirl I'll help alter them.

Mother I suppose you have to go.

Judith Ashgirl? She'll embarrass us.

Ashgirl I don't want to.

Mother If you're not there, people will say it's because I'm wicked.

Ashgirl No one will notice.

Mother Don't ever say I didn't ask you. I won't be called a mean stepmother. No one ever sees the other side.

Ruth When you meet a prince, what do you do?

Mother You get him to marry you.

Judith Why?

Mother That's what princes are for.

Ashgirl I would imagine they have their own feelings.

Mother Princes are mannequins on which young girls peg their dreams and ambitions.

Ruth My ambition is to paint. Can I paint a prince? Next to a mound of fruit?

Mother You marry him first and he'll provide all you want.

Judith Will he provide me with interesting and rare stones?

Ruth Salted hams dangling from a vaulted ceiling?

Mother One of you will marry the Prince, but you'll have to work at it, I'll tell you how as we look at my gowns. There's no time to lose.

They begin to sweep out.

Judith Rooms of marble . . .

Ruth Cakes . . .

Ashgirl remains alone.

Ashgirl Ashes . . .

SCENE FOUR
WHO LIVES IN THE PALACE

Princess Zehra's palace. It is nomadic and oriental in colour and feel: cushions, rugs, no hard furniture, a sense of luxury in the cloth as well as many books, scrolls, illuminated manuscripts.

Prince Amir, in his twenties. Dark, melancholic, anger simmering, reclines on cushions, reading.

Princess Zehra opens envelopes. A large pile is already thickening next to her.

Zehra Everyone has accepted.

Amir Since the miserable day we settled here, not one person has come to welcome us.

Zehra They're all coming now.

Amir No one has invited us. This country knows nothing of hospitality.

Zehra There are two sides to hospitality, Amir: our hosts are not welcoming, so we must be generous guests. Every girl in the region is coming to dance and some will be beautiful.

Amir No one is beautiful here, their skin is too white, they all look like boiled potatoes.

Zehra You must not speak like someone with a shrivelled heart.

Amir Are you denying they're all ugly?

Zehra You sometimes have to adjust your eyes to see beauty.

Amir You mean close them!

Zehra We haven't yet learned to find beauty in this country, we will.

Amir Never!
  Grey. Rain. Small hills. A forest with trees packed in so tight you can't even canter.
  I loved my gallops on the plains, the stars at night lancing the desert sky.

Zehra We'll become part of this country and learn to love it.

Amir I'm going back.

Zehra There's nothing to go back to.

Amir I'll find my father. If he is a prisoner, I'll free him. If he is dead, I'll avenge him and take back our pastures.

Zehra You'll find no trace of him or of our land. We are here. You will marry here and that will root you in this country. It's not the first time our family has moved to a new land.

Amir Always as conquerors.

Zehra We can still impress.

Amir I don't want to marry now.

Zehra Dance with the girls who come, Amir. A ray of beauty may emanate from one of them and soften you.

Amir I would have to forget who I am.

Zehra looks at what Amir is reading.

Zehra Why do you read poetry if you don't want to fall in love?

Amir I could not love a girl who loved this grey.

Zehra There are many ways of being a foreigner in a country: you can be exiled like us, or you can be badly treated in your own land and feel a stranger. I have seen many people here with the forlorn look of foreigners.

Amir No one here has that depth of feeling.

Zehra Beware too much homesickness my son, it's a worm that eats hope and gnaws at your strength.

Amir And why aren't you homesick at all? Why don't you ever grieve for my father?

Zehra How can you know what I feel!

Pause.

Zehra I am a mother. I owe my son a future.

Amir I may not want it.

Zehra So much anger, watch it doesn't burn you dry. Here comes Paul. Look at him, he's relinquished his anger and he is happy.

Paul comes in, also 'Indian', but expansive, more 'western'.

Paul You're giving a ball, Princess, that is an excellent and a brilliant idea. And I have learned many of this country's dances. Look, Amir: you'll like this one.

Paul begins to demonstrate.
Zehra and even Amir laugh.

Paul It's the very latest. There's a female ruler in this country who chooses her advisors according to how well they can dance, that is clever, is it not? Come and learn it, Amir, I've watched the boys in this country and modesty and restraint are out the windows. If we want to get on, we have to show off.

Amir Never!

Paul Amir!

Zehra We're only asking you to dance.

SCENE FIVE
WHO LIVES IN THE FOREST

A dark and ancient forest. Oaks, holly, ash trees. Stagnating water, ivy, black mud. The Monsters, well hidden at first, emerge from different places and heights.
First to appear, Slothworm, heavily and slowly ambling around the trunks of trees.

Slothworm I'm so tired. Always in a slump. Anyone I touch even slightly slows down too. Soon they feel so tired, they sink into a slovenly slurry of exhaustion. Can't do anything, muscles soft and sludgy, they slobber, say they're sick. They are sick, the Slothworm sickness. Slubberdegullions.

I'm sick of saying so much. Why was I asked to trudge my way through this sludge of mud to come here? I'm going to lie down on the soft ground and sink into sleep.

Angerbird flaps down from a tree, spitting angrily.

Angerbird Slothworm! Don't you dare do such a dirty trick.

Slothworm A little slumber while I wait, Angerbird, I'm sinking with exhaustion.

Angerbird I've had to flap about calling the meeting for Pridefly. Why do I always have to do all the work? Every other deadly monster in this forest is useless and it makes me very angry and if you dare close your eyes, I'll peck them out.

Slothworm Soft, Angerbird. Don't take it out on me, go and make some humans angry, provoke a war or something, I'm only a slug, a deeply sleepy slug.

Slothworm yawns, Angerbird flaps.

Angerbird What do I ever do but make humans angry, spitting, shouting, fighting, killing, but I can't make wars on my own. That's why we're having this meeting. I could have humans maiming, disfiguring, blinding and murdering each other right now.

Envysnake slithers in.

Envysnake They die anyway sooner or later, they sink rotting into the soil and worms slobber over them. They give you the credit, but it is I, Envysnake, who poison them with hatred, make them hate everybody who has something, something they haven't got, and they slink around, absolutely, sobbingly, slouchingly and supremely miserable. You've got the showy plumage – I have to slave and slither all day in this slippery skin, but I'm the one who snares those humans into that sickening, snarling envy that eats out their insides and smothers them.

Gluttontoad, fat and round:

Gluttontoad I'm hungry. I have no interest in anything except great gluts of glutinous food.

Slothworm I'm sleepy.

Gluttontoad Whoever called this meeting had better provide some glowing globules of gloaming honey for the voluminous, libidinous, cavernous stomach of this gluttonous Gluttontoad or I'm going. Who did call this meeting? Is it about food?

Slothworm Who cares?

Pridefly, small, dark, shiny and brisk, zooms on.

Pridefly I called this meeting. Who else? Would anything get done without me? We Prideflies have been here for eternity and have always done our duty with total distinction and now it falls upon me once again to shake the torpor from our midst.

Anyone can see we're not doing enough to destroy the humans. Some of them even seem quite happy and peaceful when our task is to torment them, destroy their souls and encourage their extermination. Since I seem to be the only one aware of this, I called you all here to remind you of your function and to lead you all into a new wave of human destruction.

Greedmonkey I torment them all the time. They want more and more and more. More money, more houses, more clothes, the children want more toys. People are very greedy around here thanks to the Greedmonkey, and I want more rewards for my hard work.

Pridefly There's not enough despair. What's the point of being a deadly sin if you can't wreck people's lives?

Where are the wars? The suicides? Murders in the night and disappearances? I want to see devastation all around and I have devised a strategy which only someone of my intelligence can think up.

Angerbird You don't need a strategy to make people angry. You and your meetings are beginning to annoy me, Pridefly.

Pridefly That's because you're too stupid to understand the importance of a concerted plan.

Slothworm Plan, concerted as well . . . sounds like such an effort . . .

Greedmonkey Is there a large reward? I wouldn't mind some loot.

Envysnake I never get what I deserve.

Pridefly There's a ball to be given in the palace of those new people, Princess Zehra and her son. The forest will be crisscrossed by humans off their guard. We must lie in wait, vigilant, active, aggressive. Some of us will make forays into the houses and report back on the weaknesses of our future victims. We can only enter humans through some fault in their being, and there always is one. No human must come through this forest without being pounced upon by one of us.

Slothworm Sorry, no way I'm pouncing, but I'll lie in wait . . .

Pridefly We are the Seven Deadly Sins, the monsters of the soul, the terrifying shadows of the forest, and we are here to rule the world. I will lead you as the Pridefly family has always done.

Sadness, a very human, bedraggled figure, wanders by, slowly.

Pridefly Sadness: are you with us or not?

Sadness looks at them all and glides off, slowly.

Slothworm She makes me feel even more tired . . .

Envysnake She makes my skin shiver. Why should she be so frightening?

Pridefly She acts as if she were better than us, but she's not. It's not made clear in our history and ancestry books exactly where she belongs. We're seven deadly, monstrous sins. Is Sadness the eighth monster? Something else? Leave her. She'll join us when it suits her.
Now: half of us will stay in the forest . . .

Slothworm I'm not moving . . .

Angerbird I'm off.

Pridefly And some of us will move to the houses . . .

Gluttontoad (*as he goes*) I'll go with Angerbird. I've seen plates piled with dolloping glops of gelatinous sweets in some of these houses. I could do with a mongoose mousse in couscous, followed by a Charlotte Russe and the whoosh of a bonne bouche. A spruced goose en croute infused in juiced grapefruit . . . and then . . .

Envysnake I'll wait here, I work best one to one.

Pridefly The rest of you, follow me. No slack. Let it be said in the chronicles of the future that I led the decisive battle against the humans. All for chaos and chaos to all!

*Angerbird, Gluttontoad, Greedmonkey move off, led
by Pridefly. Sloth remains and falls into a coma. Lust
comes out of the shadows and waits: a Man comes
forward, alone. Lust curls around him.*

Lust Subtle, intricate and irresistible: Lust. I am here,
always here . . .

*The Man tries to free himself. Lust laughs.
The Man falls on his knees, crying.*

SCENE SIX
WHO WORKS IN THE KITCHEN

*Heaps of materials, scraps, threads. Ashgirl measuring,
draping, cutting, pinning, sewing. The Mother rummages
through boxes of shoes and gloves. Ruth and Judith
twirl and hop in front of the mirror.*

Judith Fields of brocade.

Ruth Cascades of lace.

Judith Camelot.

Ruth Chiffon.

Judith The coolness of satin.

Ruth A drape of velvet over my shoulders.

Judith The caress of silk around my waste.

Mother Leather for the hands. Then the feet and the
problem of shoes. Too many people dress with splendour
and forget the shoes. I asked him to bring back gold
slippers from his travels. He failed. What will people say
when they see us in old shoes?

Ashgirl I can sew roses onto these shoes and add a sprig
of lace entwined with gold thread.

The Mother nods.

Judith I hate shoes, they squeeze my feet.

Mother Only peasants and animals go barefoot.

Ruth Shoes make the lady.

Mother And the lady marries the Prince.

Judith I forgot about the Prince, why do we have to marry him?

Mother Have you forgotten what he'll give you? The palaces, the clothes, shoes, furs, jewels, all yours.

Greedmonkey enters and watches.

Judith Pools of coloured stones.

Ruth Banquets.

Judith What if he doesn't want to marry us?

Mother Life will be grim if one of you doesn't marry the Prince.

Ruth Ashgirl can't marry the Prince. Ashhead.

Judith Cinderwinders, swinderbottoms, ha ha.

Mother Don't use crude language, the Prince will find you vulgar. (*to Ashgirl*) If you can make yourself a dress in time and find some shoes you can come.

Ruth You can come as our servant.

Ashgirl I don't want to go to the ball.

Ruth She doesn't want to go to the ball.

Judith She can't make the effort.

Ruth It's hard work being a girl.

Judith A marriageable daughter.

Ruth Making yourself pretty.

Judith To catch a prince's fancy.

Ruth All so you can marry.

Judith And live richly.

Ruth Ever after.

Mother These dresses don't look like anything.

Ashgirl I'll stay up through the night to make them beautiful.

Mother If your father had kept his promise and looked after us, you wouldn't have to sew the dresses

Ashgirl I'm happy to.

Ruth Happily she sews.

Judith For ever and ever.

Ruth While we marry the Prince.

Mother I see you wrapped in furs, covered in jewels, heads held high: you take your seats at the high table.

Greedmonkey joins them.

Ruth Fry an ortolan, stuff it in a pigeon, pigeon in a chicken, chicken in a goose, goose in a swan . . . I could enjoy marriage.

Judith Topaz, emeralds, pearls, rubies, sapphires, jasper, malachite and chalcedony . . . yes, I could enjoy marriage too.

The Mother throws a pair of shoes angrily at Ashgirl

Mother I'll have to wear these old shoes!

WHO VISITS THE HOUSE

Silence. A movement towards darkness.
Ashgirl remains alone.
A shadow falls suddenly across the walls. Sadness
enters, moves and tests the room for a dominant place.

Sadness The sudden hush of dusk is a good time.
Animals fall silent, ready for the night, and humans feel
alone . . .
(*Whispers.*) Ashgirl . . .
Behind a curtain, sometimes in the corner, I am the
shadow cast against the wall.
Ashgirl . . .
It's not even a sound, it's a ripple in the air, a chill in
the light, a voice they hear and do not hear.
Ashgirl . . .

Ashgirl stops working for a moment.

Young girls are easiest, but I can seep into boys too,
anyone . . . I'm the icicle in the heart, the one who
makes the world so dark you wish you weren't in it.
Sadness . . . Stretch out your hand to touch something:
all you feel is an invisible layer of cold ash covering all.
Call for help: I'll muffle your voice. Dream of relief: I'll
shrink your thoughts to dust. Don't even try to move . . .
Ashgirl . . .

Ashgirl I'll sew through the night and make these dresses
memorable.

Sadness No one will thank you.

Ashgirl The dresses will dance at the ball.

Sadness But . . . never you . . . you stay alone . . .

Ashgirl droops for a moment.

Sadness I probe, I test, study the defences and slide through the crack. An unquieted doubt, a fear, the unguarded thought . . .

(*to Ashgirl*) No one cares what you do, no one cares for you . . .

Ashgirl My father was proud of my sewing, even more proud of my writing.

Sadness He abandoned you, no one's there for you. Ashgirl, listen . . .

Owl appears at the window.

Owl Ashgirl?

Ashgirl Owl!

Sadness I hate owls!

Owl Who were you talking to? I heard a voice I didn't like.

Ashgirl I may have been talking to myself.

Owl There's a disturbance in the air . . .

Sadness You listened to me, Ashgirl. I found the breach. I won't let you go now.

Sadness moves away. Owl studies Ashgirl.

Owl You're so industrious. That means you work hard.

Ashgirl I know what it means . . .

Owl It means you work too hard.

Ashgirl You can never work too hard.

Owl Is that so? Dancing is good, too.

Ashgirl Owl, you're a serious and a wise bird, why are you always urging me to have fun?

Owl Because maybe that's serious and wise advice.

Ashgirl I don't want to go to the ball, Owl, I'm shy, like you.

Owl I'm only shy of humans. I like owls.

Ashgirl I like owls too.

Owl It's my nature to hunt alone in the night, but it is not a girl's nature to slave the night through sewing dresses.

Ashgirl When they see these dresses, they'll be so happy.

Owl And you?

Ashgirl And grateful.

Owl Will they?

Ashgirl Why do you keep asking all these questions?

Owl Wisdom is the asking of a lot of questions.

Ashgirl You're distracting me, I don't need wisdom to make these dresses perfect.

Owl Perfect dresses for your perfect sisters?

Ashgirl Owl, *I don't want to go to the ball*.

Owl Could it be you don't want to want to go to the ball?

Ashgirl I'm going to get cross.

Owl Do try!

Ashgirl Please, Owl . . .

Owl Hold one of those dresses against yourself and look in the mirror.

Ashgirl Leave me alone!

Owl No one can be happy all of the time, Ashie, but there's no harm in trying to be happy once in a while. Sometimes people don't try because they're afraid. Afraid of what? Ask yourself that. Now I must go and hunt some mice.

Ashgirl Not in this garden.

Owl I'm going to Prince Amir's garden.

Ashgirl What is he like?

Owl Why don't you see for yourself?

Ashgirl What do you think of this dress?

Ashgirl raises it unconsciously to herself and sees herself in the mirror. A moment.

Owl I only understand feathers, my dear, but I can see this dress is making you want to dance.

Ashgirl throws the dress away from herself. Owl leaves. A shadow falls.

SCENE EIGHT
WHO WAITS IN THE TREES

The forest. The Deadly Sins.

Pridefly Humans. Coming this way. Prepare to attack.

Angerbird Two young men: easy targets for me.

Slothworm (*waking slightly*) What's all the fuss?

Greedmonkey (*whispers*) Humans!

Amir and Paul come on. The sins melt into the trees.

Amir I've never liked this forest, why have you brought me here?

Paul Look at all these trees.

Amir So?

Pridefly That tone, the lift of those eyebrows.

Paul People in this country love heavy furniture made of dark wood, look at all this wood.

 The forest belongs to a baron who's off making wars. We could buy the forest, cut the trees and make furniture.

Greedmonkey Lots and lots of money.

Amir Why?

Paul Amir, we sell the furniture and become rich.

Greedmonkey Very rich. Then we buy more forests, cut down more trees and make more and more money.

Amir I have all the money I want. Do you need some?

Pridefly Our family didn't believe in commerce either. We were aristocrats, generals. Why do you keep company with such a vulgar-thoughted un-prided profit-grubbing mortal?

Paul Amir, we're in a new country, it's a good idea to have more money than you want. Furniture is the future.

Amir Our own country is in ruins and all you can think of is making furniture in this one.

Angerbird I've got them. I always knew I had the Prince, but now I can have both. Watch.

Paul We made war over there, that's all we ever did, even against each other.

Amir You've changed your name, you imitate the manners of the people here, you forget where you came from.

Paul What's wrong with that? Life is life. Land is land.

Amir How can you say that? The land you come from, the land where your ancestors were born, is not the same as this.

Pridefly Ancestors! Only the best of us have ancestors, most only have grandparents.

Amir What's happened to you?

Paul And what's happened to you? You brood all the time, you're always in a bad mood, you mope for the past. We're here, we have to survive.

Amir You were a fighter like me. Now you want to make furniture!

Paul We lost.

Amir My family doesn't lose wars. We retrench, we start again. Are you afraid of fighting?

Paul No one knows you here, no one bows down to your great family, maybe that's what you don't like.

Angerbird It's never difficult to get two young men into a fight.

Envysnake Goaded by envy, let me whisper a few words.

Amir Honour means nothing to you!

Paul They don't use that word much over here. It sounds ridiculous.

Pridefly The proud hate laughter.

The boys start to push each other.

Envysnake (*to Paul*) And if he dies, by accident here in this forest, his mother may adopt you and let you sprawl in his wealth.

The boys suddenly stop.

Amir No! Paul! My friend!

Angerbird I hate that word, I hate it! Friend. What kind of a stupid word is that anyway?

Envysnake (*to Paul*) You always have to do what he wants, he uses you, he decides, he spurs you on and then he spurns you.

Paul is still fighting. Amir folds his arms.

Amir What's happened to us? I've always hated this forest.

Paul (*stopping*) You've been more than a brother.

Amir I don't want anything to come between us.

Envysnake/Angerbird/Pridefly It will, we will make it . . .

Paul Zehra says the only two things that can come between friends are wealth . . .

Amir And marriage.

They laugh, but Amir trips over Slothworm, who attaches himself to his leg.

Paul What's wrong?

Amir I feel so weary, Paul, so weary.

Paul helps hold Amir. Kicks Slothworm away.

Paul Are you ill?

Amir Better now . . . It must have been the thought of dancing at the ball.

SCENE NINE
WHO LEAVES THE HOUSE

*The house. Ruth, Judith and the Mother in ball gowns.
Ashgirl in rags, running and fetching. No one sees them,
but things appear quickly.*

Judith Gloves.

Ruth Purse.

Judith Sash.

Mother (*to Ashgirl*) You can still come.

Judith I find this all rather silly, I'd rather be studying
rocks.

Mother Young girls must only be interested in dancing
and marriage, that's what's been agreed –

Judith By whom?

Mother By those who decide what is normal and right.
Ruth's hair is wrong.

Ashgirl fixes it.

Mother (*to Ashgirl*) Blow the candles out when we've
left: I don't want anyone to know we've left you behind.

The girls conclude last preparations.

Judith Bring me my cape.

Ruth Tie this on my nape.

Judith Fix the wrinkles on this drape.

Ruth Don't step on my crêpe.

Judith And try not to gape.

Ruth Ashie-agape.

Judith Cinders the ape.

Mother I don't like leaving you alone.
   Girls like you always make everyone feel bad, and
I think you enjoy that.

   They sweep out, followed by Ashgirl.

SCENE TEN
WHO COMES TO THE HOUSE

*Sadness comes in. Moves about and sits. Ashgirl comes
back in.*

Sadness Embers dying, the wind howls, draughts filter
through the floor, I've been waiting for such an evening.
Ashgirl . . .

   Ashgirl begins to tidy.

You can do that later. Come sit by me, Ashgirl.

   Ashgirl moves around.

We're alone, everything's quiet. We need a chat, just a
little chat, a few cold and dismal words sprinkled here
and there, those little icy words like never, alone, no one,
and then the longer, subtle ones that course through your
mind and freeze it: hopeless, friendless, voiceless, useless.
And also badness. Change a consonant and you get
my own name: sadness . . . so like madness, mad, yes,
bad . . . dad . . . add a vowel – leads to dead. I love the
way letters shift about, think how close kindness is to
blindness . . . and limpid to insipid . . .

   A scratch at the window, a high whistle . . .
   *The Otter appears, shy, furry, rather human in
   appearance, whiskers.*

Otter Psst. Ashie. Can I come in?

Sadness Another animal spoiling my plans, why are there so many animals in the world? (*She moves away.*)

Otter Humans gone? Those girls were making so much noise I could hear them from the river. You're never noisy . . . (*He puts his head on her lap.*) Let's sit quietly together and enjoy being shy.

I love ash . . .

You're more quiet than usual, Ashie, have those humans upset you?

You're thinking. Shall we think together? I love to think. What shall we think about? What were you thinking?

Ashie?

Ashgirl About a ball.

Otter That's a thought. Shall we play ball? You know I love that game. Here, catch this stone.

Ashgirl Not a ball, Otter, The Ball.

Otter What? That noisy thing that's happening at the Palace of Prince Amir. I could hear the music under the water. That's why I came here. It's not bad music, it's quite sad music, I like that, but then it got mixed in with all that noisy human laughter. It was scaring the fish away.

Much better here . . . Shall I tell you a sad story? Would you like to hear how Uncle Slim got caught in a fishing net and died?

No?

Ashie . . .

What's that noise? I hear something outside. I'll go and see. If it's a human, I'll wait till it's gone.

Otter leaves, Sadness comes back.

Sadness Only me . . . it's an old saying: always separate your prey from its friends. And now to the close.

Sadness moves around quickly, making sure all doors are closed and all candles out.

SCENE ELEVEN
WHO LIVES IN THE MIRROR

Same as before: darker. Ashgirl moves to the mirror, flickering in the semi-light.
Sadness moves close.

Sadness You do not want to go to the ball. You want to come with me.

Ashgirl If my father were here . . .

Sadness Why would he come back to you? Come to me.

Ashgirl I'll work hard, I'll grow old, one day I'll die.

Sadness Yes. Come to the ashes and we'll have a little look at death.

Ashgirl How could I go to a ball? Look at me.

Sadness Death is no worse than life, Ashie, and it's so simple . . .

Ashgirl (*to herself in the mirror, with disgust*) Look at me.

Sadness And turn away in disgust.

Ashgirl Look at me . . .

The mirror glows slightly. A voice emerges from it, clear, throaty.

Voice in the Mirror Look at yourself.

Ashgirl Who's that?

Voice in the Mirror I am in the mirror.

Sadness Don't look in there, that's vain, you have no right to be vain. Let me soothe you.

Ashgirl Who are you?

Voice in the Mirror Who are you?

Ashgirl Who am I?

    Ashgirl stares at herself. More light from the mirror.

Voice in the Mirror I am the one you find when you see yourself clearly.

Ashgirl I can't see you.

Sadness Here . . . over here . . .

Voice in the Mirror You will when you see yourself.

Ashgirl (*staring*) I'm ugly.

Sadness Yes.

Voice in the Mirror Look at yourself with clear eyes.

Ashgirl I look disgusting, horrible.

    The light begins to fade. There is a sigh.

What's happened, where are you? (*She stares.*) I'm the wrong shape, size, I'm fat.

    Darker.

Voice in the Mirror (*fading sigh*) Ashgirl . . .

Ashgirl Maybe I'm not so bad. Normal.

    A little more light.

And my eyes seem very bright.

Voice in the Mirror We can't do it all by ourselves, you have to help . . . Stand up straight and look.

Ashgirl I'm so crooked.

Groan from the mirror.

Don't go, I love listening to you . . . There, I'm almost graceful, actually, I am rather pleasing, there's something about having a body, two arms, hands, legs, it's all rather harmonious . . .

Voice in the Mirror Good. Now look at the mirror, at yourself, and see what you want.
Do you want to go to the ball? Answer the truth.

Ashgirl Yes, I do want to go to the ball, I always wanted to go the ball, but I can't, and yes, I do mind that I can't and now I'm going to be even more unhappy, I don't mind, I do mind, I don't want to be unhappy, I'm tired of being unhappy, draped in my ashcloth, I do want to go to the ball, oh, go away, I'm going to cry. I'm even getting angry.

The mirror comes to full light and the voice emerges from the mirror and stretches into a beautiful silver-clad Fairy, facets sparkling in the light. She holds a small mirror in her hand, like a fan, and she lifts Ashgirl's head gently. Sadness, blinded, melts away into the shadows.

Fairy If being unhappy makes you angry, then you can be happy.

Ashgirl Who are you?

Fairy I am the Fairy in the Mirror . . .

Ashgirl You're beautiful.

Fairy I am – even as fairies go. It's my clothes. And so are you, but it's not your clothes. Now, we don't have any time to waste. (*She takes out several silver scrolls, reads.*) I have to measure you.

Ashgirl Why?

Fairy Why? I'm not sure. Wait. I think I have the wrong page and I'm doing this the wrong way round. It's a standard recipe this. Let me see –

Ah, the animals first. I need some animals. Do you have any around?

Ashgirl Owl?

Fairy You can't do anything with owls, they have too much personality. It says you can use insects too, what about an ant?

Ashgirl Otter went into the garden. I could call him.

Fairy An otter is unusual. Will he be co-operative?

Ashgirl He's a very good friend. And then there are some mice.

Fairy Definitely. It says: always have a mouse or two at hand.

Ashgirl Otter! Come quickly, Mice!

Otter appears.

Otter Ashie, are you all right? Oh! You have company. 'Bye . . .

Fairy Stay where you are!

Otter Ashie, what's all this noise? Who's this human?

Ashgirl She's not, she's the Fairy of the Mirror.

Otter Do you have any idea how dangerous fairies are? They're always changing things, turning the world topsy-turvy. You're going to change me into something, I can see it in your face.

Fairy Stand still and stop being difficult. (*She takes out a scalpel and approaches the Otter.*)

Otter You're going to turn me into a fur coat! Ashie, this is beyond cruelty.
  Help!

  The Fairy begins to slit the fur.

Goodbye riverside, goodbye ashes, ah the sweetness of the shy and modest life. Ouch.

Fairy Am I hurting you?

Otter Not yet, but I'm a pessimist and we're always prepared for the worst. Ouch! All right, it didn't hurt, but it might have.

  She continues to scalpel, scrape, pare, as the Otter turns into a coachman, shy, bewhiskered, sniffly, but very well dressed.

Otter You've turned me into a human! That's degrading! What have I done to deserve such a punishment?

Ashgirl Otter, you look beautiful.

Otter I looked beautiful before. I'm cold.

Fairy You are the coachman, Otto. You will drive the horses and look after Ashie at the ball.

Otter And now I have to join a lot of other noisy humans at a noisy ball! I'm a creature of the river, Fairy, please let me free.

Fairy What's next? Horses . . . We need horses. Quick. Where are those mice?

  Two mice have crept in, a Girlmouse of nine and a Boymouse of five.

Girlmouse Here! Are you a good fairy or a bad fairy?

Fairy All fairies are good until they get cross. I'll only get cross if you don't do as you're told.

Girlmouse That's what everybody says.
    Hello. (*to the boy*) Say hello.
    You see how polite we are. Now I'm brave and I'm bold, I'm clever too and I know about planets and stars and I would like an adventure, please.

Fairy I'm supposed to change you into silver ponies.

Girl I'd rather be a silver dragon.

Fairy Ah – well – we don't have to do what everyone else does. You will be a silver dragon and you will be a silver pony and you will both gallop through the forest drawing the carriage. Oh! I completely forgot about the carriage. (*She reads.*) 'You may use a pumpkin.' Have you seen a pumpkin? 'Or a melon.' It's the wrong season. 'Or anything round and carvable from the vegetable kingdom.' Round. Carvable.

Ashgirl When I was a little girl I played with the shell of a walnut and pretended it was a carriage.

Fairy You always wanted to go to balls, Ashie, but then one day you lost your dream. That's the worst kind of spell. Is a walnut a vegetable?

Ashgirl It's edible.

Girlmouse A nut is a fruit. It's a seed, it's the seed of a vegetable. You may proceed.

Fairy Thank you.

Ashgirl I had forgotten that I dreamt of balls, I even painted the shell silver. That was so stupid!

Fairy Careful, Ashie: don't make me have to leave.

Ashgirl I wasted my time on dreams, I was useless.

Fairy Goodbye . . .

Boy (*to the Fairy*) Don't go . . .

Ashgirl I did keep the shell under my bed and during the day, I still keep it in my pocket, I'm so silly.

The Fairy moves away again.

Here it is.

All crowd and admire the shell Ashgirl brings out of her pocket.

Girlmouse It shines like the moon on the river.

Boymouse There are seats inside.

Otto I say, Ashie, you painted this beautifully.

Ashgirl I have no talent.

Boy She's going again!

Ashgirl It is quite beautiful.
But it's so small, how can it work?

Fairy Size is nothing to creatures of imagination.

Girlmouse Human beings think they're large, but when they look up at the stars they feel small.

Fairy Four minutes is long when you're scouring pots, but it will feel too short at the ball.

The girl and boy Mice start rampaging around the room.

Fairy Size is relative, but beauty is not. I hold something beautiful in my hand. Mice, what are you doing?

Boy Practising the gallop.

Girl I mustn't get my dragon's tail caught in the trees.

Fairy Go outside, please, and wait. Where was I?

Oh you spirits of imagination, come to my help now –
Something beautiful in my hand, something beautiful in
my mind – matter shifts under the power of wish, shapes
itself to the image sparkling in the mind, feeds on the
desire for existence and – a thing of beauty emerges in
the garden.

I think I've done it!

A carriage in the garden.

Fairy Now to the most difficult item, your dress.

Ashgirl I can sew.

Fairy I can change matter, but not the cruel rush of time.
The ball has started, we need the original dressmakers of
the early world, we need the spiders.

*The spiders begin to climb down from ropes. There
are quite a few of them and Ashgirl screams.*

Ashgirl But I'm afraid of them.

Fairy No magic without courage.
Let them measure you.

The spiders measure, work quickly.

Fairy They want to know what kind of a dress you
want.

Ashgirl Anything . . .

Fairy A spider's web?

Ashgirl I want something beautiful, shiny, slinky, silvery,
watery, glittery, dangly, jangly, tingly, glossy and fleury.

*Light silver cloth, layer upon layer: Ashgirl finds
herself dressed and draped in a mirrory silver dress,
long, elegant, sparkling.
The Fairy turns her to the mirror.*

39

Fairy You know the story, don't you? There once was a proud girl who boasted she could weave more beautifully than anyone on earth or in the heavens, she was so proud she claimed she was better than the ancient goddess Athena. So they had a contest, which Athena won, but Athena was so cross with her she punished her by turning her into a spider. You girls are the opposite, you're not proud of anything, you're terrified of admitting you do anything well. I'm not telling you to boast, but when you say you're no good, everything you do is rubbish, you become so annoying we fairies may end up turning you into spiders as well. We may not even have to do it to you: you do it so well to yourselves.

Now you may look at yourself.

Ashgirl It isn't me.

Fairy It is you.

Ashgirl It is.
I am here.
I am beautiful.

Fairy At last: the transformation of the heart begins.

Ashgirl Let's go, Otto, I'm ready, I can't wait. Suddenly the future looks like a pile of precious stones, which my hands long to gather. Let's go!

Fairy Wait!

Ashgirl It was a dream . . .

Fairy Not a dream, but magic. And magic cannot last because it is a chance and chance is short and fleeting. There is another magic that might last, but it depends on you. For the moment, know that the carriage, the dragon and the pony, Otto himself and your clothes cannot move through the twelfth bell of midnight. Why? Because time buries chance and no fairy has ever diverted its ruthless rhythm. We try. Sometimes we cheat by a few years, once we managed a hundred – I was there. Where was I? Here. Now. You must return home before midnight. Otto and Owl will warn you. Do not forget – return home.

Ashgirl To my old life?

Fairy If you let chance change you, no. Now go.

Ashgirl Can you not come with me?

Fairy I breathe your reflection, I must live in the mirror. Sometimes you'll find me in water. Don't forget my words.

Ashgirl What made you come to me tonight?

Fairy Yourself. Go . . .

Ashgirl I am beautiful and I am going dancing.

Fairy A girl is always beautiful when she is going dancing.

Act Two

SCENE ONE

Zehra's palace. Reds and golds, flowers. Sense of plenty and hospitality. Zehra, Paul and Amir greet guests as they come in. Then a farandole forms, led by Paul. A dinner bell rings, and Zehra leads everyone out.

Only Amir remains behind, plucking idly at an instrument, melancholic. He sinks in the cushions and remains unseen when Ashgirl arrives.

She bursts in, resplendent in her silver dress and cloak. Otto follows, very twitchy, takes her cloak. Ashgirl centres herself in the seemingly empty room.

Ashgirl I've missed the dance!

Otto They've all gone into supper. I can hear the noise.

Ashgirl I've missed what I most wanted.

Otto Let's go home.

Ashgirl You'll have to dance with me.

Otto I only like river music.

Ashgirl This music is like a river, listen.

Otto And coachmen don't dance, it's not dignified.

Ashgirl takes Otto by the hand and makes him dance. He is not happy.

We could be having such a good time in the ashes. And these human bones are aching. You'll have to dance by yourself.

Amir emerges from the cushions, smiles at Ashgirl and takes her hand. They dance easily, a formal Renaissance dance, look at each a little and keep dancing, unable to speak.

Ashgirl (*out*) I'd like to say: I love dancing with you –
but I don't want him to know I've never danced with a boy before.

Amir (*out*) I'd like to say: I love dancing with you –
but I don't want her to know how much I'm enjoying being with her.

Ashgirl I'd like to say: please stay with me all evening –
but I don't want him to think I'm too stupid to talk to anyone else.

Amir I'd like to say: come in to dinner with me and sit with me –
but I don't want her to know she's the only girl I want to talk to.

Ashgirl I'd like to say: it's so beautiful here –
but I don't want him to know I've never been anywhere so full of light and colour, even though it's true.

Amir I'd like to ask: where have you come from? Why so late? And without parents –
but I don't want her to think I'm so interested, even though I am.

Ashgirl Should I leave? I want to stay.

Amir Should I stop dancing? I want to go on.

Ashgirl I can't say anything: he must think I'm stupid.

Amir She must think I'm a cretin.

They look at each other, each holds a hand out to the other.

Ashgirl/Amir (*over each other*) What's your name?

They laugh. Pause.

Ashgirl/Amir (*over each other*) Amir. Ashgirl.

They laugh.

Amir Where have you come from, Ashgirl?

Ashgirl (*out*) I can't tell him about now, but I could about before . . .
(*to Amir*) I had a pony when I was little.
(*out*) Why did I say that!

Amir There are wild ponies where I come from. Great festivals too.
(*out*) What a stupid thing to say.

Ashgirl We had music and flowers in our house.
(*out*) He's going to think, so what?

Amir We raced ponies over the plains.
(*out*) Why can't I stop talking about horses!

A pause.

Ashgirl I'm tongueless, mute, unvoiced. Fairy of the Mirror, change this silence into words.

Amir I can fight battles, I've never feared death, but I'm too afraid to say anything to her.

Ashgirl/Amir I loved dancing with you!

Amir Come in with me to have dinner.

Ashgirl Yes! I'm so hungry.

Ashgirl starts at what she's just said then moves off with Amir. Judith and Ruth come on, food in their mouths, and collapse on the cushions.

Judith You eat, you dance, you get hot, you get bothered, you get tired, you get bored, it's such hard work marrying a prince, I'm going home.

Ruth Mother said one of us has to marry this prince.

Judith What will she do if we don't?

Ruth When Mother is disappointed I feel like I'm going to shrivel into a speck of dust.

Judith With me it's more like feeling strangled.

Ruth She loves us and wants everything for us.

Judith I don't want everything, I only want a microscope.

The Mother storms in.

Mother Why aren't you two sitting next to the Prince?

Ruth He has that girl in silver next to him and only talks to her.

Mother Move in. You only have one night to marry this prince. I'll send him this way: don't disappoint me.

Zehra comes in.

Zehra Are the young girls all right? They left the banquet.

Mother They're delicate and need a little quiet.

Zehra Shall I ask the musicians to play something soothing?

Judith No! Your music's boring.

Mother We live very quietly, grandly, very grandly, but quietly. Silence will do. My daughters work so hard at their accomplishments . . .

Zehra Indeed, and these are?

Mother Everything feminine.

Zehra Ah?

Pause.

Ruth I cook and I eat – I paint too.

Zehra So does Amir. He likes to paint scenes of our wars and of our land.

Ruth I like violence too, I paint things that rot, with flies.

Zehra My son paints heroism, shall I send in some food?

Ruth Yes! Syrupy cakes. And a slice of marzipan from Turkistan . . .

Mother And they would so enjoy speaking to your son.

Zehra Of course. Paul, where is Amir?

Paul I keep looking for him, I am doing all the dancing, (*to the girls*) I will dance with you.

Judith Do you have a title?

Paul Yes, I have been the fastest rider and soon I will be the fastest dancer. I will dance with the oldest daughter first, as is courteous.

Ruth We mean: are you a prince or a duke or something?

Mother My daughters will wait quietly for your son, Princess.

The Mother sweeps Zehra out. Paul follows.

Judith What do you do to marry a prince?

Ruth You kiss him and then you marry him. If he kisses you, he has to marry you, those are the rules.

Ashgirl and Amir come in, talking.

Amir I don't know where my father is . . .

Ashgirl Mine told me he had to leave . . .

Amir We had many enemies . . .

Ashgirl My father spoke of enemies within.

Amir Everything is so different here . . .

Ashgirl It all changed when he left.

Amir I never feel at home . . .

Ashgirl I have to tell you I'm not what I seem . . .

Amir Sometimes I'm no longer sure of who I am . . .

The sisters begin to move in.
Owl appears at the window.

Ashgirl I have to go.

Amir Please not yet . . .

Ashgirl I want to stay . . .

Judith and Ruth close in, finger Ashgirl's dress.

Amir I want to ask you . . .

Ruth Where did you find all those little mirrors?

Judith What makes your hair sparkle so?

Ruth Can I look more closely at your shoes?

Ashgirl keeps trying to move away. Otto comes in,
flustered, shaking, Owl hoots.

Amir Tell me who –

Judith What are these precious stones on your bracelet?

The clock strikes and Owl hoots. Otto dangles
Ashgirl's cloak.

Ashgirl I have to go.

Amir Tell me where –

Owl hoots.

Judith That's strange, you have ash in your hair.

Amir Let me know who you are!

Ruth, turning towards Otto, lets out a scream.

Ruth That man is holding a giant spider's web in his hands!

Ashgirl flees, with Otto following.
Amir tries to go after her, but Judith and Ruth circle around him singing a child's game.

Judith/Ruth
Round the green gravel the grass is so green
And all the fine ladies that ever were seen
Washed in milk and dressed in silk
The last that stoops down shall be married –

Ruth picks up Ashgirl's shoe, throws it to Judith who throws it back.

Judith/Ruth
There's a lady on a mountain
Who she is I do not know
All she wants is gold and silver . . .

Amir I would like that shoe.

Ruth throws it to Judith. They get frantic.

Judith/Ruth
Choose to the east, choose to the west,
And choose the one that you love best.

Amir Please have the kindness to give me that shoe.

Ruth
If they're not here to take their part
Choose another with all your heart.

Judith (*stops dancing*) I will give it to you: in return for a kiss.

Judith dangles the shoe.

Do you want the shoe or not?

Amir kisses her quickly, but she holds on to him.

Judith You kissed me and now you marry me.

Ruth Those are the rules.

They start singing again.

Judith/Ruth
She kissed him, she hugged him,
She sat upon his knee
She said, dear Prince, won't you marry me

Amir rushes out with the shoe.

Judith I'm not sure I want to marry him.

Ruth Then you should have let me kiss him, now you have to obey the rules.

SCENE TWO

The forest, dark and threatening. Ashgirl in torn rags and black spider threads. Tormented by what's on her.

Ashgirl I was at the ball. It wasn't me. I'm covered in mud. Spiders in my hair. Who was there? Where was I?

A Man emerges from the trees.

Man Got you!

Ashgirl Let me go!

Man Later. Maybe.

Ashgirl What do you want?

Lust comes and joins them.

Lust (*to the Man*) All you know is that you want and here is a chance.

Man Come with me.

Ashgirl Where?

Lust (*laughs*) Into the deepest and darkest part of the forest.

Man (*looking at Ashgirl*) You're so young! (*He hesitates. To Lust*) No. I can't. Let me go! Please! Have pity.

Lust When have lust and pity ever mixed? I am what I am – and I have you.

Ashgirl (*to the Man*) Who are you talking to?

Man The monster I can no longer fight!

Lust Here, everywhere, in any shape, in her shape.

Ashgirl You seem – who are you?

Man (*laughs*) I can't remember.

Lust Late one night, a man worked hard in his study. He looked up and he saw me. He tried to read, he tried to cry.

Man She's a child!

Lust An object. Why object?

Ashgirl (*to the Man*) You are so like – the laugh – not exactly the same, but –

Lust No one remains what they were when I pass through them.

> *Ashgirl and the Man stare at each other. The Man pushes Lust away.*

Man (*to Lust*) Siren-voiced fiend. I won't let you drag me down – not to this.

> *The Man runs off, screaming. Lust pursues, laughing.*

Lust He tried to pray, he tried to run.

Ashgirl remains still.

Ashgirl Father? Father . . . (*She calls.*) Father!

Sadness approaches. The other Monsters also begin to close in, but silently, watching Sadness at work.

Father . . . I don't understand . . .

Sadness You have no father.

Ashgirl He loved me, he protected me What happened?

Sadness He found something better.

Ashgirl Where am I? Who am I?

Sadness Nowhere, no one . . . alone . . .

Ashgirl I was at the ball, I'm sure I was at the ball.

Sadness If you were at the ball, I was there too.

Ashgirl I danced.

Sadness I don't remember.

Ashgirl It was so beautiful. And so was I.

Sadness Look at yourself: ashes, covered in spider webs.

Ashgirl I wore silver.

Sadness Look around, Ashgirl, feel the world as it is.

Slothworm creeps up.

Slothworm Aren't you tired? Aren't your limbs feeling heavy and slow?

Ashgirl Please . . .

Sadness This is what you get from your sisters.

Angerbird You take up too much room, we don't want to see you, *shrink*!

Sadness Don't cover your eyes. Their mother . . .

Pridefly We had respect, you brought us down.

Angerbird You and your father!

Pridefly People without names!

Ashgirl He was kind at the ball, we ate together.

Gluttontoad You ate? Mounds of molten meats? Fluid rivulets of fetid fat revolving and dissolving in the oleaginous omasum of an omadhaun . . .

Sadness (*over*) You knew the world was like this, that's why you hid in the ashes. What arrogance made you want to come out? This is what you find.

Lust caresses Ashgirl.

Lust I wrapped myself around him . . . I threaded through the sinews of his sober heart. He can never escape.

Ashgirl struggles.

Ashgirl Help me!

Sadness This is the world where screams go silent.

A figure appears, wrapped in a dark cloak. Ashgirl screams.

Figure There you are at last.

Ashgirl No! No! No! Please –

Otter Ashie, what's the matter, it's me, Otto, I mean Otter. I've been looking for you, I've never been in this part of the forest – we must get to the river and then I'll know the way out –

Ashgirl There's no way out . . .

Otter We have to get out of these trees.

Ashgirl I don't know how . . .

Otter Ashie, quick, I sense danger, and when I sense danger I have to run, it's instinct, I can't help it. Run with me.

Ashgirl I can't.

Otter I'm beginning to shake, that means I have to run, Ashie, take my paw.

Ashgirl Leave me here . . .

Otter I smell danger, can't you feel it? I'm frightened, I have to run, my heart is beating, my feet twitching ! Save yourself!

Otter runs off. Sadness from the trees.

Ashgirl I can't move . . .

Slothworm There's safety in paralysis.

Gluttontoad Sweet and sticky the trickle of sugary syrup on your breath.

Sadness You're here. Mine.

Owl hoots.

Ashgirl Owl?

Sadness There's no owl, it's in your mind, your mad mind.

Owl hoots.

Owl (*distant*) Ashie . . .

Ashgirl Where are you?

Owl Over here, in the moonlight, at the edge of the forest.

Sadness There's no edge, there's no moonlight, there's no way out of the forest.

Ashgirl: frozen in terror, shaking.
  The two Mice scurry on.

Girlmouse Help! Ashie, help us. We're so frightened and we're lost and I'm not a dragon any more.

The children start crying and throw themselves on Ashgirl.

Boy She's cold.

Sadness Turned to stone. Leave her . . . run along.

Girlmouse Ashie, can you hear us? If you don't help us, we'll be lost for ever.

Sadness And if you don't run soon, this toad will eat you.

Girlmouse Toads don't eat mice and we're more frightened of owls. I can feel a heartbeat.

Sadness Not for long . . .

Girlmouse Ashie, we're your friends and you're our only hope.

Ashgirl makes a final effort to extricate herself.

Ashgirl Hope . . .

Sadness They're mice, Ashgirl . . . mice. Mice!

Girlmouse What's wrong with being a mouse?

Boymouse Mice are nice and have no vice.

Ashgirl smiles, gets up. The Mice take her hands. The Monsters vanish.

Owl At last, you're safe.

Otter Let me dry you with my fur.

Ashgirl Where were you all when I needed you?

Owl In the forest, dear girl, you need yourself.

The house. Ruth. Judith. Ashgirl.

Ruth We were surrounded.

Judith Admired.

Ruth We danced with the Prince.

Judith And he chose me.

Ashgirl He didn't!

Ruth Were you there?

Judith The Prince kissed me.

Ashgirl He couldn't have.

Judith Were you there?

Ruth She made the Prince kiss her.

Judith He wanted to kiss me.

Ashgirl He did not want to kiss you.

Judith Were you there?

Ashgirl Yes! No! I can imagine.

Judith Then you can imagine me kissing the Prince. He's going to marry me.

Ashgirl He isn't!

Judith You know him?

Ashgirl In my imagination.

Ruth He only wanted the shoe.

Ashgirl The shoe?

Judith There was this stupid-looking girl and she lost her shoe.

Ashgirl She was beautiful!

Ruth You were there?

Ashgirl The shoe –?

Judith Princes are shy, the shoe was an excuse.

Ashgirl It stayed as a shoe? It didn't change?

Ruth It was an ugly old shoe to begin with.

Ashgirl It was not!

Ruth Were you there?

Judith I'd have to cut off half my foot to get into that measly titchy witchy ugly shoe – it was what we call a preliminary – it began the kiss.

Ashgirl But the shoe stayed as it was?

Ruth The shoe's not part of the story. We're marrying the Prince – well – Judith is marrying him and I'm going to all the parties.

Ashgirl He'll never marry Judith.

Ruth You'll stop him?

Judith Dance with him?

Ruth Kiss him?

Ashgirl Why not! – In my imagination.

Ruth Then you can marry him – in your imagination.

Judith No! Not even in her imagination. I'm marrying him, no one else. Say: I wasn't there.

Ashgirl Leave me alone.

Ruth Say it: I wasn't there.

Ashgirl I can't do anything about my imagination.

Judith Then I'll have to open up your head and cut it out.

Ruth You had better say you were not there.

Judith In any shape, form, image or -ation.

Ruth Say it!

Ashgirl Maybe I wasn't . . .

SCENES FOUR AND FIVE

The palace and the house. Amir, Paul and Zehra in the palace. Ashgirl alone with the mirror in the other.

Zehra How do you know she was more than a spirit of the air?

Paul I made a list of all the girls who came and of their parents and of their wealth, and there is no one on this list by that name.

Amir She was there. She was human.

Zehra It's not easy to tell who is human, there are so many imitations.

   Ashgirl in the hearth.

Ashgirl I wasn't there. It wasn't me.

Amir I looked at her, I knew I wanted to marry her.

Zehra You cannot marry a girl who vanishes into the night.

Ashgirl Where was I if I wasn't there?

Paul At the top of the list, I have put the five wealthiest and most beautiful girls for you, Amir. Portraits are being sent.

Zehra She must have been a serving girl with stolen clothes.

Paul What I like about the girls in this country is their hands are so soft, they are so wealthy they do nothing all day. Did you look at her hands?

Amir They were strong, that's what I liked.

Ashgirl And I'm hungry all the time. Hungry for him. Hungry.

Zehra I have to announce your choice or the whole country will be offended.

Paul They'll say you think no one is good enough for you.

Zehra You have to marry.

Amir I cannot love anyone else.

Zehra I said marry, I wouldn't pry into your heart.

Amir You're asking me to marry without love.

Zehra We all fall in love with a dream, we wake up one day anyway and find ourselves living with a stranger. Marriage is learning to live with that stranger.

Amir I touched her hands. I remember how they felt.

Ashgirl We talked, we laughed, we held hands. I remember.

Amir I have to find her.

Zehra How can you find a spark that's gone out?

Amir takes out the shoe.

Amir I have this.

Ashgirl And the shoe never changed. I was there.

Zehra studies the shoe.

Zehra Mirrors, gossamer threads finely webbed. There is beauty here, Amir, but what can you do with a shoe?

Amir I don't know . . . I don't know!

Zehra I have to advise you to be sensible. Falling in love with a shoe is not wise.

Paul I think Amir should obey his mother and marry one of the girls at the top of the list, that's what I would do.

Ashgirl The shoe didn't change, the other shoe is buried somewhere in the mud of the forest.

Paul Even if she existed, you'll never find her again.

Zehra And she won't be the one you remembered from a whirling evening. How could she be?

Ashgirl In the mud. What can I do? Nothing. Was I ever even there?

I'm so tired . . . Time to bury the dreams . . .

Amir You've worn me down. Show me the list. Or choose yourself.

Ashgirl In the ashes.

Amir Leave me now: I have battles to plan . . .

Ashgirl and Amir both go still and listless.

Ashgirl Amir . . .

Amir Ashgirl . . .

Fairy of the Mirror Ashgirl . . .

Zehra Amir . . .

Fairy of the Mirror Ashgirl . . . don't waste time . . .

Zehra I can give you three days, no more, to find this girl and bring her to me. I will ask her questions that will make her reveal who she is.

Fairy of the Mirror The shoe didn't change, find the shoe.

Amir How am I going to find her?

Zehra That's your quest: you have a shoe.

Ashgirl In the forest! I can't go back.

Amir I can hardly ask every girl in this land to try on a shoe!

Ashgirl I'm afraid, please . . .

Fairy of the Mirror Look into yourself, find your courage.

Paul It is a very good way of meeting families, I'll come with you.

Amir I'll be laughed at.

Zehra Being laughed at is an excellent preparation for marriage.

Fairy You can't love without courage.

Ashgirl Life was so safe in the ashes.

Amir She distracts me from my plans . . .

Amir and Ashgirl stretch out their hands to each other.

Amir/Ashgirl When we touched . . .

Ashgirl I couldn't tell my fingers apart . . .

Amir My hand melted . . .

Ashgirl . . . from his.

Amir . . . into hers

The Fairy hands a silver cloak to Ashgirl.

Fairy of the Mirror Take this cloak, it will help you find your way.

Zehra wraps a coat around Amir.

Zehra This will keep you warm: beware the shadows of the forest.

SCENE SIX

The house. The sisters and their Mother. Ruth is working a piece of cardboard.
Greedmonkey explores the room.

Ruth It was even smaller.

Judith It couldn't have been smaller.

Ruth I'm an artist, I remember these things. (*She cuts.*)

Mother Put your foot on it.

Judith does so, they all stare.

Mother How did you get such big feet? I told you not to walk so much.

Ruth It's the big toe that doesn't fit.

Mother Yes. Only the big toe.

Pause.

Do you need it?

Greedmonkey becomes attentive.

Judith Need what, Mother?

Mother Your big toe. Is it of any use?

Judith It's my big toe.

Pause.

Mother Without it, the shoe would fit.

Pause. Greedmonkey whirls.

Palaces, clothes, jewels, wealth, power.

Ruth Not just you, either: your family. I could paint with gold and silver. I'd paint your portrait. Next to a big white cake.

Greedmonkey mimics.

Mother People would bow down to us as we passed. At grand feasts, we'd stand tall in our finery and all would try to catch a glimpse of us, beg for a kind word, cringe for one of our smiles.

Ruth If only you didn't have those toes.

Mother Without them, you'd be a princess! A grand princess.

Judith Yes, but I do have toes.

Mother At the moment.

Pause.

There's a country I know where young girls have all the bones of their feet broken to look beautiful. These are only big toes.

Judith I don't understand . . .

Ruth The shoe would fit.

Mother I've always thought toes ugly.

Judith I like them, they're mine.

Mother Especially big ones. They're just not dainty, are they?

Judith I don't even want to marry the Prince! (*to Ruth*) You marry him!

Ruth You kissed him.

Judith What are you going to do?

Mother There's a woman on the edge of the forest who knows how to add a little flesh here, take away a few bones there, all for the sake of beauty. How else can a woman have power? We'll seek her advice.

Judith About what?

Mother You'll see. It's all for your own good.

Judith I'm not going.

Ruth You have to! Girls don't disobey their mothers.

Mother I'll be there. Looking after you.

Judith I don't want to see an old woman who does things to the body!

Mother We'll only ask her advice.

Ruth Time to stop snivelling and act like a princess. Imagine all the things you'll have to play with in the palace.

Judith You won't let her hurt me?

Mother You won't mind anything when you feel gold run through your fingers.

Greedmonkey turns out, leading the three behind him.

Greedmonkey It's so easy to deal with humans. All you have to do is give them images: bright pictures of gold, houses, jewels, clothes, food, and they follow you like slaves. No human can resist a tempting picture: they look, they want. Gold for you, madam, sweets for you, my girl, what about a palace? Here's a picture of you wearing furs, silk. A slide-show of wants: Want – want – want more, and now, they follow me – Pied Piper of tempting images, playing the jaunty jingles of greed.

The forest. Monsters.

Angerbird A disturbance in the air. Cruelty, anger, hatreds rage through the world. Turbulence and confusion drive waves of humans hither-thither, inexorable fear in their dark minds. The humans are converging towards the forest tonight, we must seize our chance and be alert.

Slothworm Alert? I have to be alert?

Envysnake Alert. Subtle. So easy to pour the smooth poison of envy into those soft human veins. The heart seizes up, the mind splutters and spits and their spirit smothers in sourness. So: alert.

Pridefly There's nothing more alert than a fly, you know. Do you know how many famous alert flies have graced the pages of history? Poems, ballads, short stories have been written about us, even in French.

The animals, alert, try to hush the fly.

Monsters The Prince!

Pridefly I see the Prince. Who do you think brought him here?

Amir and Paul, weary and dejected.

Amir Three hundred and seventy-five feet. And when I looked up, faces convulsed in greed and giggles.

Amir sits – it happens to be on top of Slothworm.

Slothworm My motto has always been: all comes to the one who does nothing.

Envysnake (*to Paul*) You've tried three hundred and seventy-five shoes on three hundred and seventy-five feet with him and what has he done for you? And the girls never even looked at you.

Amir And not one of those girls made my heart beat faster.

Slothworm Listen: girls are a Big Effort. Not worth it.

Envysnake (*to Paul*) All your life, you've looked after him and now you're exhausting yourself running after his dream. But you're still on your own struggling to get rich. Does he help you?

Amir (*to Paul*) Shall we go home?

Pridefly (*to Amir*) You'll never find anyone to match you, Prince. This is a country of shopkeepers, that's one of my best sayings; you can quote me any time.

Paul (*to Amir*) If you wish.

Slothworm (*to Amir*) Much better to lie in soft cushions than trudge around the countryside on a rainy day.

Paul (*to Amir*) There are a few more houses on the other side of the forest.

Pridefly The wrong side of the forest.

Slothworm Why bother?

Envysnake Always helping him. Why?

Amir She was a dream . . .

Slothworm Best if she stays that way, that way you can dream about her and have a sleep at the same time. That's what I call romance.

Paul I believe, like your mother, she was a serving girl who tricked you.

Pridefly Mocked princes soon become tarnished objects of boredom.

Paul Princess Zehra will find you a suitable wife and you'll be content.

Amir That may be enough for you! I don't want to be content!

Paul (*angry*) Some of us would be grateful for that much. I don't have parents looking after me, worrying about my happiness, I don't have anything, but you can't stop complaining!

Amir Paul . . . why so angry? Everything I have has been yours to share.

Paul/Envysnake I don't want to share! I want it all for myself!

> *Crashing through the trees, whimpering – the Mother appears with the two girls and Greedmonkey. Judith is hobbling and crying.*

Mother We heard you were making your way to all the houses, but we thought it best to come and meet you: here is your wife, Prince Amir.

> *A moment.*

Amir I do not recognise her.

Mother Men have no memories for faces. The shoe will fit.

Amir (*to Judith*) What did we talk about?

Mother How can a girl remember what a prince said to her?

Amir The girl I remember would remember.

Mother You proclaimed you would marry the girl whose foot fits the shoe. Do people in your country not keep their word?

*Paul kneels down and puts Judith's foot in the shoe.
She writhes in pain, but the shoe goes on.*

Paul The shoe fits.

Mother The shoe fits.

Ruth The shoe fits.

Amir There is one other condition: the girl whose foot fits the shoe must come back and answer three questions put to her by my mother.

Ruth An exam, we're good at exams! Can I come too?

Mother (*to Judith*) Go with the Prince.

Judith Now? On foot?

Mother Have you not provided a carriage for the Princess?

Amir She is not a princess yet and it is not far.

Paul She seems in pain.

Amir Perhaps the shoe does not fit?

Mother The shoe fits. Now please give her a pledge of your love.

*Amir reluctantly offers a ring. Judith looks at it,
dejected.*

Mother Take her to the palace, Prince, and show her around her new home.

*Ashgirl comes on, covered in mud. She sees Judith and
the Prince. She reaches out, about to speak, but Sadness
covers her mouth.
Amir, Paul and Judith go off hurriedly. Mother and
Ruth leave in a different direction. The Monsters melt
into the forest and watch.*

SCENE EIGHT

Ashgirl He left with her. He forgot me.
　It was all for nothing.
　I tried to call him when he passed by, mud and ashes
came out of my mouth.

*She holds the mud-covered shoe. Sadness stays very
still, watching.*

Ashgirl Fairy of the Mirror . . . you were never there . . .
　Amir . . . Illusion.
　It was all for nothing.

Lust Desire coiled around him . . . I held him fast . . .

Ashgirl Where do I go now? Mud and ashes . . .

Lust All strength worn away. Lost in the forest . . .

Ashgirl This endless forest . . .

Slothworm Endless . . .

*Screams and sobbing in the distance. Ashgirl moves
off, Sadness following on her heel.*

SCENE NINE

*The forest: the Monsters move forward, Angerbird
prominent.
　Darkness.
　Amir and Paul drag Judith on. She is crying, hobbling,
bleeding heavily. Angerbird hovers.*

Amir Cheat. Liar. False.

Judith Your evil mother did this to me asking those
stupid questions. I stamped my foot and this!

She shows her blood-soaked foot.

68

Amir You never felt love.

Judith What does love have to do with it? You're rich. I'm supposed to marry you!

Amir I despise you!

Judith You're not much to look at yourself.

Paul Why go to such extremes?

Judith My mother told me to.

Amir The cunning in your mother's eyes.

Judith She's better than yours, that witch waiting in the forest.

Amir I will not trade insults with you. Paul will take you home.

Judith Leave me here, both of you. I don't need you. (*to Paul*) That goes for you too, Footboy.

Envysnake Footboy!

Amir You've made me despise women.

Judith How do you think I feel about men!

Paul leaves. Angerbird wraps Judith.

Angerbird She made you cut off your foot for an idiot. You never felt such pain. Your mother lured you, betrayed you, your sister laughed when the old woman sliced off your toe. What is there left for you now but hatred and revenge? Rage, girl, rage, try to make someone else suffer as you have, that's the kind of anger I like, an anger that spreads like a forest fire through crackling dried trees. Rage, Judith, rage.

The Monsters surround Judith.

Judith I hate this world. I hate, I hate – I hate everyone. I hate everything.

Mother and Ruth come on. They see Judith.

Mother Judith!

Judith Don't ever talk to me again.

She lunges for her mother.
The Mother sees the blood.

Mother He found out!

Judith How could you do this!

Mother I wanted only what was best for you.

Judith Not this, never this! Look at me.
I can't walk!

Mother I didn't make the world, Judith. What else could I do?

Judith Mother: I'm mutilated.

Mother It will be worse if we don't save the situation.

A pause. The Mother and Judith look at Ruth.

Ruth No! No! Please! No!

Judith Oh yes, yes, yes. Now you'll see what it feels like to help your family. Oh yes.

Mother We have to, Ruth, or we'll be disgraced, we'll be turned into beggars!

Ruth No!

Mother I never liked this harsh world, but we have to survive. There's no time to lose – you have to help us.

Ruth No! Help me, someone, please!

Judith Obey your mother!

Ruth tries to escape, but is caught by the Mother and Judith, who drag her off. Ashgirl comes on with Sadness at her heels. Screams in the distance. Screams, sobs. Ashgirl stands still.

Ashgirl Where are you?

Sadness Here.

Ashgirl Yes.

Sadness You're tired, aren't you?

Ashgirl Yes . . . the screams . . .

Sadness If you sleep you'll only hear my breathing.

Ashgirl So cold . . .

Sadness I'll wrap you in my arms.

Ashgirl Nowhere to go . . .

Sadness Lay your head on my shoulders.

Ashgirl Yes.

Sadness Lie down, it's so quiet here, no sounds, no memories . . .

Ashgirl Amir . . .

Sadness Who?

Ashgirl I don't know.

Sadness Turn your face towards the mud . . . down.

Ashgirl The Fairy's cloak . . .

Sadness Let me put my cloak over your head . . . I'll keep the world quiet, you'll never feel pain again . . .

Ashgirl The shoe . . .

Sadness There's such peace without memory, turn your head to the mud. Do you really need to breathe?

The Monsters approach. Sadness motions them to be quiet.

Shh. I think I have her.

Fairy's Voice Ashgirl . . .

Ashgirl What was that?

Sadness The wind in the trees. Rest now. Turn your head back down, down to the mud. You've had enough . . .

Ashgirl Yes . . .

Fairy's Voice If you fall asleep, you'll never wake up.

Sadness And so? Sadness in every breath. Ugliness. Sleep . . .

Monsters Sleep . . .

Fairy Find your courage, Ashgirl . . .

Sadness What's courage but a stupid rush into more knocks and pain? Who needs the horror of the world, Ashgirl? Sleep.

Monsters Sleep . . .

Fairy Look into yourself.

Sadness Remember the darkness that surrounds your life.

Fairy Look into your heart, Ashie, and remember your courage.

Sadness The cruelty of your sisters.

Fairy The animals who made you laugh.

Sadness Days and nights shivering in the ashes.

Fairy Dancing at the ball.

Sadness Always alone, shunned.

Fairy The warmth of shared words . . .

Sadness You caused suffering.

Fairy Find your hope . . .

Sadness Where did hope lead?

Ashgirl When we danced: ashes . . . no, when we danced, light . . . I was that girl, happy, ashes . . . no, I was hungry, happy, and I could give: suffering, no, the pleasure of my company, I looked at myself. I saw: spiderwebs, no, the glitter of possibility, what I could be, ashes . . . no, I was . . . nothing . . . no, I see: mud, no, I see light coming through the trees, illusion, don't look, no, beauty in the world . . .

Fairy In myself.

Sadness Too late, let me sleep.

Ashgirl Too late.

Sadness Too much.

Ashgirl Too sad.

Sadness Nothing.

Fairy One good memory.

Sadness No reaction. I have her.

Ashgirl I can remember . . .

Fairy When you slept out in the woods with your father . . .

Ashgirl I searched for words to describe the first light.

Fairy Fragile, filigreed . . .

Ashgirl I could never catch the words, but I felt . . .

Fairy/Ashgirl Joy . . . strength . . .

Dawn has filtered into the forest, rain washes the muddied cloak, Ashgirl rises covered in the cloak.

Ashgirl I know who I am and I will be what I am.

Sadness Spite, fury and gloom. I've lost her!

Ashgirl I'm not afraid of the shadows of this forest, nor of myself, nor of the future.

The Fairy appears.

Fairy I've been so frightened for you.

Ashgirl I know there is darkness, I've seen the monsters of the forest, but I'm not afraid.

Fairy I couldn't come to you until you came to yourself.

Ashgirl I will never be afraid . . .

Amir comes on. Stares at Ashgirl –

. . . of asking you to remember . . .

Amir I heard your voice . . . I sensed your presence.

Ashgirl I came looking . . .

Amir I searched the muddy pools, I held on to my memory . . .

Ashgirl For you . . .

Amir Of . . .

Ashgirl I knew despair.

Amir I lost hope. It is you?

Ashgirl Your hands . . .

They hold their hands. The Mother comes on with Ruth.

Mother Prince! Here is your bride. (*She laughs.*) My girls are like twins, they always play these tricks. It was never Judith, it's this one. The shoe fits Ruth!

Prince I have found the one I love.

The Mother sees Ashgirl.

Mother What are you doing here? Go back home at once! (*She laughs wildly.*) She's the embarrassment of the family, a girl with a father we can't mention, we take pity on her and feed her, she's full of tricks, her father's a criminal who ran away into the forest – Go. Disappear! shamed child of a shamed father. She won't deny her father's shame!

A moment. The Man emerges from the forest.

Man I'll deny it. I'll deny every word you've uttered.

Ashgirl Father . . .

Man I have been caught in the claws of a most terrible monster. I live in the forest and fight daily. I cannot free myself yet, but there are no crimes . . . I have come close – but there are no crimes.
  (*to Amir*) This child is a brave child, Prince. I don't know her heart now, but I knew it well when she was little.

Ruth (*to her Mother*) You cut off my heel for nothing! It's infected! I'll never walk again!

Ruth cries out in agony. Judith limps forward.

The Man (*to the Mother*) How could you do this to your daughters?

Mother I did what I had to. I was always told only wealth mattered, and I must do what I could to acquire it. I only

75

ever did what I was told. Where were you when we needed you?

Fairy (*to the Mother*) These are your own daughters: where was your love and your compassion?

Mother Love? Compassion? How could I ever learn those words? Whoever had love and compassion for me? Keep up appearances, that's what I was taught, crave power, grasp riches, I was told. Love and compassion rotted underneath. I only ever did what was done to me.

The Mother lifts her skirts to reveal her own stumps. The father bows his head. The Fairy turns to Ashgirl.

Fairy Will you have the courage to change this circle of cruel convention?

Amir We will change everything.

Ashgirl With you . . .

Paul appears, stops them.

Paul Not yet. Princess Zehra has sent me to tell you to do nothing until she has spoken.

Amir I know my own heart.

Paul holds a sword. The Monsters watch with interest.

Paul Amir: your mother has given me the power to make you do as I say. You will wait.

SCENE ELEVEN

Change of light. Zehra appears, regal, in full dress, very formal. She stands tall and turns to Ashgirl. The Mice come on and watch intently.

Zehra You will answer my questions.

Amir Mother, this is my bride –

Zehra Not yet.

Amir I know her.

Zehra But I do not.

Judith She'll never be able to answer the questions!

Mother The shoe still fits Ruth.

Amir Mother, I will not allow your questions.

Zehra You promised.

Paul You do not break promises, Amir.

Ashgirl Fairy of the Mirror, don't let me lose everything now.

Fairy Remember yourself and you will answer the questions.

Zehra (*to Ashgirl*) Come here. Closer.
  Why do you love my son?

  Ashgirl doesn't answer. A moment.

Amir Surely you can answer that.

  Ashgirl stays silent.

Judith She can't even answer the first question!

Zehra Here is my second question:
  Will you love my son for the rest of your life?

Amir That's easy.

Ashgirl stays silent.

Ashie, please: say yes!

Silence.

Zehra My third question is:
Will you always be able to wear the silver shoes you wore at the ball?

Silence.

Mother Ruth could answer all those questions.

Amir Please answer my mother!

Ashgirl stays silent. A pause. Judith and Ruth smirk.

Zehra Come here, child. Here is my son: I wish you great happiness.

Amir I don't understand.

Zehra How can you say why you love someone? A thousand reasons crisscross the heart, but at the centre – no reason at all, only the mystery of that person. If you say you love someone because they are rich or handsome or powerful, you love only a fraction. She knew this.

Will she love you for the rest of her life? It is you, Amir, who must make her love you as she will make you love her. Neglect her, treat her badly, you will kill her love. Never sit back lazily waiting for love to take care of itself, tend it, cherish it.

As for the shoes: perhaps they will fit, perhaps not. She will change. She will not want you to ask her to wear shoes that were beautiful once but no longer feel like hers. Never ever ask her to cut off her foot to fit a shoe from the past.

The questions could not be answered. Your future wife knew this.

Fairy My work is almost done. (*to the Mother*) I have to change you into something horrid.

Mother I followed the rules. They were the wrong rules, but I had no way of knowing that. We're taught to obey and when we obey the wrong rules we're blamed. Do what you want with me, I no longer care.

Fairy I'll change you into an ash tree under which nothing grows. You'll stay in the forest.

Paul Which I will cut down. One day, you'll be a piece of furniture.

The Mother shrugs.

Fairy As for you girls, when your mother asks you to do something stupid and harmful have the courage to say no. It is difficult, I know, and I won't be harsh. Choose your own punishments.

Ruth I want to live alone and never see anyone again.

Fairy I'll turn you into a hermit who lives in a cave.

Ruth I'll paint the carcasses of dead animals.

Judith I want to stay in the forest and study rocks and leaves and map the inside of the earth, it's all I ever wanted to do.

Fairy And now to you, Ashgirl: you too will change, move, search, but first you must live this part of your story and conclude it. Come here, Ashgirl, who sought and found her heart and her courage.

The Father (*to Ashgirl*) I did not want to remember my name in the forest. And so I had forgotten yours too . . . but now I can give it back to you: your mother and I named you Sophia – because it is an ancient word for wisdom.

Lust comes on.

Lust I found him in his study –

The Father I cannot stay, the Monster calls, but when I triumph – and I will triumph – I'll find you again, my child. (*to Zehra*) Will you help her understand?

Zehra She will understand.

He goes back into the forest. Zehra now wraps a beautiful cloth around Ashgirl and Amir. The Fairy helps. The Monsters begin to move and exit.

Angerbird What is it about these humans that makes them so strong?

Envysnake What do they have we can't break?

Slothworm Energy?

Pridefly Friendship swats the prideflies every time.

Greedmonkey I'm leading them in my dance and suddenly, they stand still, reach out their hands and break the spell with one dazzling gesture of generosity.

Envysnake It makes my venom powerless, it is called hope.

Sadness hovers over Zehra for a moment.

Zehra (*to Sadness*) I know you, but not now . . . (*to Amir and Ashgirl*) We have stilled the forest.
It is your time now . . .

Amir and Ashgirl, wrapped in each other.

Ashgirl I was always looking for –

Amir I searched, I kept searching –

Fairy Seize now the glitter of these moments –

Ashgirl It was a ray of memory –

Amir I remembered your hand –

Fairy The never forgotten sparkle –

Ashgirl Even when I believed I'd lost you.

Amir It was never a dream, I knew you were there –

Fairy The rare flash –

Ashgirl I searched, and I found –

Amir I knew I could find –

Ashgirl You –

Amir You –

Fairy Of happiness.